D0596789

Doggie Delights & Kitty Cuisine

Taste-tested by Cinnamon

by Martha Ward

Martha Ward and

Copyright © 1997 Martha Ward

First Edition

ISBN 0-9658993-0-6

All rights reserved. Reproduction in whole or in part of any portion in any form without permission of publisher is prohibited.

Library of Congress Catalog Card Number: 97-061078

Published by
Bow-Wow Books
Wautoma, Wisconsin 54982

Illustrated by
Gene Malasics

Printed in the United States of America by
Palmer Publications, Inc.
318 North Main Street
PO Box 296
Amherst, Wisconsin 54406

Designed and marketed by
Amherst Press
A division of Palmer Publications, Inc.
PO Box 296
Amherst, Wisconsin 54406

Dedication

Cinnamon Ward
1983-1997

Doggie Delights and Kitty Cuisine: Taste-tested by Cinnamon was inspired by Cinnamon's love of homemade pet treats and sampling them, even treats made for cats. After giving enthusiastically received bones and cookies to friends and relatives, we put the recipes in a book. Cinnamon, then nearly 14, spent her life's twilight months as "official" taste-tester. She probably thought she was in doggie heaven before she actually was. The book is dedicated to Cinnamon and her love of homemade, gourmet pet treats.

Contents

Acknowledgments

For the encouragement, advice, guidance and information given to us as novice authors, we thank the following friends and family members: Richard, Susan, Jeffrey, and Kay Ward, Roger Gale, Chris Halla, Linda Leighton, Judy Kohn, J. C. Hirt, Ross Mueller, Kathy Bronk, and all those who contributed recipes. We would also like to thank the Palmer Publications staff.

For illustrations that nuzzle our funny bones, we thank our artist friend, Gene Malasics.

For serving as excellent taste-testers and advisors, we thank our animal friends: Allegro, Arthur, Bear, Cajun, Ginger, Kitty, Lacey, Nick, Shadow, and Zoey.

Cinnamon Ward

Martha Ward

Introduction

"Treats!" When I hear that word, I come running faster than any golden retriever you've ever seen! With a name like Cinnamon, I was probably destined to enjoy tasting. Since I am nearly 14 years old in people years, I'm an experienced taster.

We live out in the country, and I have a good life. When the weather is nice, my people-dad takes me for boat rides on the lake, and I like to fish under our pier. Almost every day I go jogging with my people-mom. If I stay with her, she gives me a treat when we get home.

My favorite treat times are very snowy winter days. On blustery, stay-at-home days, my people-mom often bakes special gourmet pet treats, and I assist her by sampling them. That is the best tasting task!

At holiday time we gave homemade goodies to our animal friends and relatives. People and pets thought the treats were great, and several wanted to make them at home. My people-mom and I decided to share the recipes of Doggie Delights and Kitty Cuisine in a book. We hope everyone has as much fun making and sampling pet snacks as we do.

Getting Started

Creating pet treats is not difficult and doesn't require a lot of time. The number of ingredients needed is small, and equipment and methods are uncomplicated. This is an activity that is fun for adults and children to do together. Its mixing and shaping methods (using the hands, like with play dough) are even good for developing hand and finger strength and dexterity. The treats produced are enthusiastically welcomed by pets.

Ingredients

Many ingredients in dog and cat treats are available in the grocery store or may already be in your cupboard:

Baby food, strained vegetable and meat

Bouillon powder

Buttermilk or dried buttermilk mix

Eggs

Garlic powder

Onion powder

Powdered dry milk

Rolled oats (quick, not microwave)

Unbleached flour

Vegetable cooking oil

Wheat germ

Whole wheat flour

Other ingredients enhance taste, texture, and the variety of treats:

Brewer's yeast (available in pet stores)

Brown rice

Canned meat and seafood

Corn

Carob chips

Carrots

Catnip (available in pet stores)

Cheese (Cheddar and Neufchatel)

Honey

Molasses

Nuts

Potatoes

Sesame seeds

Spices (ginger, cinnamon, etc.)

Sunflower seeds

Variety flours (soy, rye)

Wheat bread crumbs

Whole grain cereal

Recipes may call for special ingredients such as apples, yogurt, or noodles, so it is best to check the ingredients required for a recipe before beginning to work on a particular treat.

Pureed chicken liver and broth may be prepared by cooking chicken livers in water (simmer 1-1 ½ hours). Puree in a food processor or mash with a fork or potato masher. Mix with broth until the consistency is similar to mashed potatoes. Store in small containers (4-8 ounces) in the freezer until needed.

Utensils

Treats require only a few utensils and actually can be mixed and patted out using one's hands. Having these utensils would be helpful:

Can opener

Cookie cutters (available at kitchen gadget, craft, or
   variety stores)

Cookie sheets

Cutting board

Food processor or electric mixer (may be used but is not
   essential if you mix by hand)

Large mixing bowl

Measuring spoons

Rolling pin

Small baking pan

Small bowls

Spatula

Spoons, forks, knives

Mixing Methods

Usually recipes follow a routine of mixing dry ingredients together and then liquid ingredients together before combining them. While an electric mixer may be used, the authors prefer mixing with hands (similar to play dough mixing), or with a food processor. A fork or wooden spoon may also be used. If the mixture is sticky, a small amount of nonstick cooking spray may be sprayed on the hands and utensils to make mixing easier.

Baking

Most recipes call for treats to be cut in shapes or strips, etc., and baked on cookie sheets sprayed with nonstick cooking spray. Bones and cookies may also be shaped "free form" by hand. Some doughs are spread in small baking pans which have been lightly greased. For those, cutting is done after baking.

Conventional oven baking is recommended.

Crunchy, dry treats are especially good for a pet's teeth.

Cooling a baked bone or cookie treat in the oven with the door closed will add to its crunchiness.

Storage

Since these healthy treats do not contain preservatives, they are best stored in the refrigerator or freezer. Most may be placed in plastic bags when cooled, and they will maintain their freshness for 6-9 months in the freezer. Those stored in the refrigerator should be used within two weeks.

Doggie Delights

An Apple a Day

If these make me healthy, wealthy and wise, I'm on the program for good!

Yield: 2-2½ dozen treats

2 cups whole wheat flour	1 egg, beaten
½ cup unbleached flour	⅓ cup cooking oil
½ cup cornmeal	1 tablespoon brown sugar
1 apple, chopped or grated	⅔ cup water

Preheat oven to 350 degrees. Spray cookie sheet with nonstick cooking spray. Lightly dust work surface with flour.

Blend the flours and cornmeal in a large mixing bowl. Add the apple, egg, oil, sugar and water; mix until well blended. On floured surface, roll dough to a ¼-inch thickness. Cut with cookie cutter. Place treats on prepared sheet. Bake 35-40 minutes. Turn off oven. Leave door closed 1 hour to "crisp" treats. Remove treats from oven. Store baked treats in an airtight container or plastic bag and place in refrigerator or freezer.

Cookie cutters shaped like a doggie bone or fish are available at most kitchen gadget, craft, or variety stores. Bones and cookies can also be shaped "free form" by hand.

Makin' Bacon

I love it when my people-mom makes BLT sandwiches. That means bacon goodies are on the way for puppies too!

Yield: 2½-3 dozen treats

¼ cup powdered dry milk
½ cup unbleached flour
½ cup whole wheat flour
¼ cup cornmeal
3 slices bacon, fried and
      crumbled

2 tablespoons bacon
      drippings
2 eggs, beaten
½ cup water

Preheat oven to 350 degrees. Spray cookie sheet with nonstick cooking spray.

Combine dry milk, flours and cornmeal in a large mixing bowl. Add bacon, bacon drippings, eggs and water; mix well. Drop by ½ teaspoonful on prepared sheet. Bake 25 minutes. Turn off oven, leaving door closed to "crisp" treats. Remove treats from oven. Store baked treats in an airtight container or plastic bag and place in refrigerator or freezer.

Like most dogs, I don't like storms. When I hear thunder, I head for the basement. I feel better when my people-mom brings doggie delights and comes down too.

Cinny's Favorite Cookies

Honey and cinnamon make these morsels as delicious as my name.

Yield: 3-3½ dozen cookies

1 cup rolled oats	2 eggs, beaten
½ cup wheat germ	¼ cup honey
1 cup unbleached flour	¼ cup cooking oil
½ teaspoon cinnamon	¼ cup milk

Preheat oven to 350 degrees. Spray cookie sheet with nonstick cooking spray.

Mix oats, wheat germ, flour and cinnamon together in a large mixing bowl. Add eggs, honey, oil and milk; blend well. Drop by teaspoonful on prepared sheet. Bake 15 minutes. Remove treats from oven and cool on a wire rack. Store baked treats in a plastic bag and place in refrigerator or freezer.

Once, I interrupted our jog around the lake to visit a church picnic near our house. I am thinking of joining; they gave me cinnamon cookie treats.

Catch the Rye

Jeff, my people-brother, taught me to "Catch the Rye" by flipping it up after he put it on my nose. One-quarter cup cornmeal and 1/4 cup unbleached flour may be substituted for the soy flour.

Yield: 2-2½ dozen treats

2	cups rye flour
½	cup soy flour
6	tablespoons cooking oil
⅔	cup warm water

Preheat oven to 350 degrees. Spray cookie sheet with nonstick cooking spray. Lightly dust work surface with flour.

Blend flours together in a large mixing bowl. Combine oil and water and hand mix with flours. Roll to a 1/4-inch thickness on floured surface. Cut in desired shapes with cookie cutter and place on prepared sheet. Bake 40 minutes. Remove treats from oven and cool on wire rack. Store baked treats in a plastic bag and place in refrigerator or freezer. (These freeze well.)

Hand mixing is just that. Because pet treats don't contain much oil, it is often easiest to mix ingredients together using one's hands, as would be done with play dough or clay.

Chicken Delight

A spoonful of sugar makes this a delightful treat for any time of day!

Yield: 4-4½ dozen treats

4 cups unbleached flour	2 cups hot water
3 cups rolled oats	4 tablespoons cooking oil
2 tablespoons brown sugar	1 egg, beaten
2 chicken or beef bouillon cubes	

Preheat oven to 325 degrees. Lightly dust work surface with flour.

Blend flour, oats and sugar in a large mixing bowl.

In a separate bowl, dissolve bouillon cubes in hot water. Let cool. After bouillon mixture cools, add oil and egg. Mix well. Add bouillon mixture to flour mixture and mix by hand until all ingredients are moistened.

On floured surface, roll dough to a ¼-inch thickness. Cut in desired shapes, using your favorite cookie cutters. Bake on ungreased cookie sheet for 1 hour. Turn off oven, leaving door closed and leave treats in to "crisp" overnight. Remove treats from oven. Store baked treats in a plastic bag and place in freezer.

If the dough mixture is sticky while hand mixing, a bit of vegetable oil may be sprayed or rubbed on hands to reduce sticking.

Can't Believe It's Not Chocolate

Allegro says closet chocolate-lover dogs will adore these "decaffeinated" goodies!

Yield: 3½-4 dozen treats

3	cups unbleached flour	1	cup water
½	cup wheat germ	¼	cup cooking oil
2½	cups rolled oats	¼	cup carob chips
1	tablespoon brown sugar	¼	cup molasses
½	cup powdered dry milk		

Preheat oven to 300 degrees. Spray cookie sheet with nonstick cooking spray.

Blend flour, wheat germ, oats and sugar in a large mixing bowl.

In a large sauce pan, mix dry milk in water. Add oil, carob chips, and molasses to milk/water mixture. Heat over low heat until carob chips are melted. Remove from heat and add to dry mixture; blend until all ingredients are moistened.

Roll dough on greased counter or prepared sheet. Cut into desired shapes with cookie cutter. Bake 1 hour. Remove treats from oven and cool on a wire rack. Store baked treats in an airtight container or plastic bag and place in refrigerator or freezer.

Most dogs like chocolate, but it is not recommended for them because it contains caffeine. Carob is a tasty and acceptable alternative.

Eat Your Wheateez

Do I jog faster after a few of these, or is it that I am hurrying home for a refill?

Yield: 2-2½ dozen treats

2½ cups whole wheat flour	1 tablespoon molasses
¼ cup wheat germ	¼ cup milk
1 teaspoon garlic powder	1 egg, beaten
½ teaspoon salt	¼ cup cooking oil

Preheat oven to 375 degrees.

Combine flour, wheat germ, garlic powder and salt in a large mixing bowl.

In a separate bowl beat together molasses, milk, egg, and oil. Blend into dry mixture until all ingredients are moistened. Add a small amount of water if needed to shape into a ball. (Dough should be stiff.)

Roll to a ½-inch thickness; cut into desired shapes with cookie cutter. Place treats on ungreased cookie sheet. Bake 20 minutes. Remove treats from oven and cool on a wire rack. Store baked treats in an airtight container or plastic bag and place in refrigerator or freezer.

My people-mom, Martha, goes jogging each morning, usually around the lake. I go, too! This is great! I see nice people and smell good smells, and if I am good, I get a treat when we get home.

You Are My Sunflower

My cousin Lacey loves these! She will grow the sunflowers in her garden for seeds if we will make the cookies.

Yield: 2½-3 dozen cookies

2 cups whole wheat flour
½ cup soy flour
¼ cup cornmeal
1 teaspoon brewer's yeast
¼ cup sunflower seeds

2 eggs, beaten
¼ cup milk
2 tablespoons cooking oil
¼ cup molasses

In a small bowl, mix eggs with milk. Reserve ¼ cup of egg/milk mixture. Add oil and molasses to the remaining egg/milk mixture and mix well. Combine with the flour mixture; blend well. Knead the dough 3 minutes; let it rest 1 hour.

Preheat oven to 350 degrees. Spray cookie sheet with nonstick cooking spray.

Roll dough to a ½-inch thickness. Cut or shape into desired shapes using cookie cutter or hands. Brush with reserved egg/milk mixture. Place treats on prepared sheet and bake 30 minutes. Cool in oven to increase crispness. Store baked treats in an airtight container or plastic bag and place in refrigerator or freezer.

Resting is when a kneaded ball of dough is loosely covered with a cloth or wax paper and left to sit for a period.

Cheeseheads

Put on your Packer-backer kerchief and chomp away on this fantastic treat!

Yield: 5 dozen triangles

1 cup grated Cheddar cheese
  (room temperature)
1/3 cup margarine, softened
1/3 cup milk
1 cup whole wheat flour
1 cup unbleached flour
1/2 teaspoon garlic powder

Cream cheese by beating it with margarine in a large mixing bowl. Mix in milk. Blend in flours and garlic powder. Form into a ball and chill 1/2 hour.

Preheat oven to 375 degrees.

Roll dough to a 1/4-inch thickness and cut into 1-inch triangles using a cookie cutter or knife. Place on ungreased cookie sheet. Bake 15 minutes. Remove treats from oven and cool on a wire rack. Store baked treats in a plastic bag and place in freezer.

Grated cheese should be at room temperature when a recipe is mixed. This produces a smoother dough.

Grin and Bear It

My cousin, Bear (who is actually a golden retriever), says these are so good and so good for you that a little garlic-breath is tolerable.

Yield: 2 1/2-3 dozen treats

1 cup unbleached flour
1 cup whole wheat flour
1 cup powdered dry milk
2 teaspoons garlic powder

2 eggs, beaten
1/4 cup honey
1/4 cup cooking oil
2 cups water

Preheat oven to 350 degrees. Spray cookie sheet with nonstick cooking spray.

Blend flours, dry milk and garlic powder in a large mixing bowl. Add eggs, honey, oil and water. Mix until all ingredients are moistened. Roll out with rolling pin to a 1/2-inch thickness. Cut with cookie cutters or shape with hands. Place treats on prepared sheet and bake 25 minutes. Turn off oven and let treats cool on sheet in oven. Remove treats from oven. Store in an airtight container and place in freezer.

Since the dough for treats is often "stiff", a food processor works better than an electric mixer for combining ingredients if cooks don't care to "hand mix."

Macarena Meatloaf

Who said meatloaf is boring? I'd do the Wave and the Macarena for this! Ground turkey or venison may be substituted for ground beef.

Yield: 1 loaf (12 slices)

1 cup cooked brown rice
1 pound ground beef
2 eggs, beaten
1/2 teaspoon salt
1/2 cup whole wheat bread crumbs
1 jar (2 1/2 ounces) strained vegetable baby food
  (peas, carrots or green beans)

Preheat oven to 350 degrees. Spray 9x9-inch pan with nonstick cooking spray.

Mix rice, beef, eggs, salt, crumbs and baby food in prepared pan, using hands. Form into loaf. Bake 45 minutes. Remove loaf from oven. Slice and crumble to serve. Store meatloaf in an airtight container and place in refrigerator.

*My people-dad, Dick, likes to nap on the couch. So do I.
When he asks me to move, I pretend I am asleep. When he
says, "Treat?" I make room for him immediately!*

Ginger Snaps

"You'll snap these up no matter what your name is," says my neighbor, Shadow.

Yield: 2½-3 dozen treats

2½ cups whole wheat flour
½ cup powdered dry milk
1 teaspoon salt
1 teaspoon sugar
½ teaspoon ginger

½ cup cool water
1 egg, beaten
6 tablespoons margarine, softened

Preheat oven to 325 degrees. Spray cookie sheet with nonstick cooking spray.

Blend flour, dry milk, salt, sugar and ginger in a large mixing bowl.

Mix water, egg and margarine together in a separate bowl. Add to dry mixture and mix until all ingredients are moistened. Knead by hand to form a ball. Roll with a rolling pin to a ¼-inch thickness. Cut or shape with cookie cutter or by hand.

Place treats on prepared sheet. Bake 12 minutes. Remove treats from oven and cool on a wire rack. Store baked treats in an airtight container or plastic bag and place in refrigerator or freezer.

Kneading refers to working mixed dough with the hands and heels of the hands to press, stretch, and roll the dough, increasing the uniformity of the mixture.

Open Sesame

These crunchy cookies will "open the door" for good things such as standing still for grooming.

Yield: 3½-4 dozen cookies

1¾	cups unbleached flour	½	cup cooking oil
¼	cup wheat germ	½	teaspoon lemon juice
⅓	cup packed brown sugar	½	teaspoon vanilla extract
¼	cup sesame seeds	1	egg, beaten
½	cup ground nuts		

Blend flour, wheat germ and sugar in a large mixing bowl. Add sesame seeds and nuts; blend. Add oil, lemon juice, vanilla, and egg. Mix well, using hands. Form into 5-6 log-shaped rolls. Chill for 1 hour.

Preheat oven to 375 degrees.

Using knife, slice dough into ¼-inch-thick round pieces or shape as desired with hands. Bake 10-12 minutes on ungreased cookie sheet. Remove from oven and cool on a wire rack. May be frozen as logs and then thawed, sliced and baked at a later time. Store baked treats in an airtight container or plastic bag and place in refrigerator or freezer.

Lots of times I am bathed in our lake. I don't really like this much, but if I am cooperative, the family gives me doggie bones when we are finished—a fitting reward!

This Little Piggy

This little piggy will bring you a wonderful treat, whether he goes to the market or not! (Kittens like these too!) Beef, lamb or chicken baby food may be substituted for pork baby food.

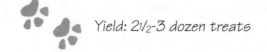

Yield: 2½-3 dozen treats

1	jar (2½ ounces) strained pork baby food
½	cup powdered dry milk
½	cup wheat germ
¼	teaspoon garlic or onion powder
2	tablespoons milk

Preheat oven to 350 degrees. Spray cookie sheet with nonstick cooking spray.

Mix baby food, dry milk, wheat germ, garlic powder and milk together in a large mixing bowl. Form small balls or drop by ½ teaspoonful on prepared sheet. Bake 10-12 minutes. Remove treats from oven and cool on a wire rack. Store in an airtight container or plastic bag and place in refrigerator or freezer.

If crispier treats are preferred, this and almost any other bone- or cookie-type treat may be left in the oven to cool, with the door closed, after it is turned off.

Let Them Eat Cake

Get out the party hats! It's birthday time, and here comes cake for all my pals!

Yield: one 8-inch round cake (18-24 wedges)

3½ cups whole wheat flour
2¼ cups rolled oats
3 tablespoons brown sugar
2 cups water
3 tablespoons cooking oil
¼ cup carob chips

Preheat oven to 300 degrees. Spray 8-inch round baking pan with nonstick cooking spray.

Mix flour and oats in a large mixing bowl. In a medium saucepan, mix brown sugar, water, oil and carob chips together. Heat over low heat until chips are melted. Add to flour mixture; mix well. Spoon mixture into prepared pan. Bake 1½ hours or until firm to the touch. Remove pan from oven and cut into small wedges to serve. Store in an airtight container or plastic bag and place in refrigerator or freezer.

Sometimes when I am outside and am called, I dilly-dally about going home. When the call is "Doggie Bones," I am home in a flash!

Show Me the Honey

Party! Party! We'll eat this cake for my birthday and play
"Doggie, doggie, where's your bone?"

Yield: one 9x9-inch square cake (16 pieces)

1 cup whole wheat flour	1 egg, beaten
1/2 cup soy flour	1/4 cup cooking oil
1 teaspoon baking soda	1 teaspoon vanilla extract
1/4 cup finely chopped or	1/3 cup honey
ground peanuts	1 cup grated carrots

Preheat oven to 325 degrees. Spray 9x9-inch baking pan with non-stick cooking spray and lightly dust with flour.

Combine flours, soda and peanuts. Mix in egg, oil, vanilla, honey and carrots until well blended. Pour into prepared pan. Bake 20 minutes. Remove from oven and cool. Cut in squares. Store baked treats in an airtight container or plastic bag and place in refrigerator or freezer.

When my people-brother Jeff was little, I liked to lie on the floor beside his chair at the dinner table. That's where the most crumb-treats fell.

Licken' Good Chicken

This is paw-licken' good grub! Are seconds available?

Yield: 3-3½ dozen treats

2 cups unbleached flour	1 egg, beaten
1 cup cornmeal	3 chicken or beef bouillon cubes
2/3 cup wheat germ	
1½ teaspoon garlic powder	1½ cups hot water
½ teaspoon salt (optional)	

Preheat oven to 375 degrees. Spray cookie sheet with nonstick cooking spray.

Mix flour, cornmeal, wheat germ, garlic powder and salt together in a large mixing bowl. In a separate bowl, dissolve bouillon cubes in the water. Add egg and bouillon mixture to flour mixture; mix well.

Roll dough to a ½-inch thickness. Cut or form in desired shapes using cookie cutter or hands. Place treats on prepared sheet. Bake 20 minutes. Remove treats from oven and cool on a wire rack. Store in an airtight container or plastic bag and place in refrigerator or freezer.

When my people-mom works at the kitchen counter, I lie on the floor beside her. Who knows when she will make a "mistake" and drop a treat on the floor as she packs them in bags?

Crystal Lake Crunch

This canine version of trail mix would be great after jogging around the lake!

Yield: fourteen 1/4-cup servings

2 cups rolled oats	1/4 cup sesame seeds
1/2 cup coarsely chopped bran cereal	1/4 cup sliced almonds
1/2 cup wheat germ	1/4 cup honey
	1/4 cup cooking oil

Preheat oven to 225 degrees. Spray 13x9-inch baking pan with nonstick cooking spray.

Blend oats, cereal, wheat germ, sesame seeds and almonds together in a large mixing bowl. Spread evenly in prepared pan. Combine honey and oil in a small saucepan. Heat on low heat to melt honey. Pour over dry mixture; mix well. Bake 1½ hours, stirring every 15 minutes. Remove pan from oven and cool on a wire rack. Store mix in an airtight container or plastic bag and place in refrigerator or freezer.

I like the water at our lake. We used to have a paddle boat and I rode in front—sort of like a hood ornament. My favorite boat is the little pontoon boat—I can go for a boat ride and take a nap at the same time.

Herky Jerky

Prime snacks for top dogs! Hide these from your people-dad!

Yield: 24 strips

$\frac{1}{4}$ cup salad oil
$\frac{1}{4}$ cup soy sauce
$\frac{1}{4}$ teaspoon garlic powder
1 tablespoon brown sugar
1 pound beef, lamb, venison or ham steaks

In large mixing bowl combine oil, soy sauce, garlic powder and sugar. Cut beef, lamb, venison or ham into $\frac{1}{2}$-inch strips. Add to bowl and marinate 1 hour.

Preheat oven to 175 degrees. Spray cookie sheet with nonstick cooking spray.

Place strips on prepared sheet and bake 5 hours with the oven door slightly ajar. Remove jerky from sheet and cool. Refrigeration is not needed. Store jerky in an airtight bag or container. These may be frozen.

If I have a treat that I really love, I crawl under the coffee table in the living room to eat it. That way, no one will bother me.

Live It Up with Chicken

My people-mom doesn't like chicken liver, so I reap rewards with these munchies.

Yield: 40-50 strips

½ cup pureed, cooked
    chicken liver*
1 cup chicken broth
½ cup powdered dry milk
1 tablespoon brewer's
    yeast

1 cup soy flour
3 cups whole wheat flour
1 cup rolled oats

Preheat oven to 350 degrees. Spray cookie sheet with nonstick cooking spray.

Mix liver, broth and dry milk in a large mixing bowl; set aside. In a separate bowl mix yeast, flours and oats. Add to liquid mixture, blending until all ingredients are moist. Roll or pat out to a ¼-inch thickness. Cut in ¼-inch strips and place strips on prepared sheet. Bake 20 minutes. Remove treats from oven and cool on a wire rack. Crumble to serve. Store baked treats in an airtight container and place in freezer.

To make pureed, cooked chicken liver, mash cooked chicken liver using a potato masher or fork. Add broth until the mixture is the consistency of mashed potatoes.

Take a Whiff!

Here's a sure cure for "dog breath." I don't know if it works for people.

Yield: 2-2½ dozen treats

2 cups whole wheat flour
½ cup cornmeal
1 teaspoon mint extract
¼ cup cooking oil
½ cup water
1 tablespoon dried, minced parsley, crumbled

Preheat oven to 350 degrees. Spray cookie sheet with nonstick cooking spray.

Combine flour and cornmeal in a large mixing bowl. Add mint extract, oil, water and parsley; mix well. Roll to a ¼-inch thickness and cut with cookie cutters. Place treats on prepared sheet and bake 40 minutes. Cool in oven. Store treats in an airtight container or plastic bag and place in refrigerator or freezer.

Since I have learned that good behavior yields treats, I have abandoned all thoughts of visiting Mr. Kinsey's compost pile down the road.

Mighty Good Meatballs

I have a ball with these little gems—makes me decide not to snatch my people-mom's golf ball.

Yield: 2-2½ dozen balls

½ pound ground beef
1 small carrot, grated
1 tablespoon grated
   cheese
¼ teaspoon onion powder

½ cup whole wheat bread
   crumbs
1 egg, beaten
1 tablespoon tomato
   paste

Preheat oven to 350 degrees. Spray cookie sheet with nonstick spray.

Combine beef, carrot, cheese, onion powder, bread crumbs, egg and tomato paste in a large mixing bowl. Mix by hand or with fork. Form into ¾-inch balls. Place balls on prepared sheet. Bake 15 minutes. Remove pan from oven. Place pan on wire rack; cool. Store in an airtight container or plastic bag and place in refrigerator or freezer.

Using 100 percent whole wheat bread crusts, whole wheat bread crumbs can be easily made in a food processor and stored in the freezer.

Health Nut

I'm nuts about these! How can anything so good for you taste so great?

Yield: 2½-3 dozen treats

2½ cups whole wheat flour	¼ cup ground or finely chopped nuts
½ cup powdered dry milk	1 egg, beaten
½ teaspoon salt	⅓ cup cooking oil
¼ teaspoon garlic powder	1½ cups cold water
1 teaspoon brewer's yeast	

Preheat oven to 350 degrees. Spray cookie sheet with nonstick cooking spray.

Combine flour, dry milk, salt, garlic, yeast and nuts in a large mixing bowl. In a separate bowl, mix egg, oil and water; add gradually to dry mixture, blending well. Roll out to a ¼-inch thickness and cut or shape as desired using cookie cutter or hands. Bake 30-45 minutes. Remove treats from oven and cool on a wire rack. Store baked treats in an airtight container or plastic bag and place in refrigerator or freezer.

Nuts used in pet treats should be unsalted. They may be coarsely chopped or finely ground in a food processor or purchased already prepared.

Feel Your Oats

All my canine friends will gallop home for these terrific bones!

Yield: 5½-6 dozen treats

6	cups whole wheat flour
5	cups rolled oats
1½	cups powdered dry milk
2	eggs, beaten
2	cups cooked hamburger or pureed, cooked chicken liver with broth
3	tablespoons molasses

Preheat oven to 350 degrees. Lightly dust work surface with flour.

Mix flour, oats, dry milk, eggs, hamburger and molasses together in a large mixing bowl. Add enough warm water (1-1½ cups) to make a very stiff dough. Roll out to a ¼-inch thickness on floured surface. Cut in desired shapes using cookie cutter or knife. Bake 20-30 minutes. Remove treats from oven and cool on a wire rack. Store baked treats in an airtight container or plastic bag and place in freezer.

Oatmeal or rolled oats used in pet treats may be "quick" or "regular" but not "microwave."

Peanut Butter Pups

My people-friend Grace says Zoey loves peanut butter. These are for all the puppies who are peanut butter lovers!

Yield: 3-3½ dozen treats

3 cups whole wheat flour
½ cup rolled oats
½ cup powdered dry milk
2 teaspoons baking powder

1²/₃ cups milk
1½ cups creamy peanut butter
2 tablespoons molasses

Preheat oven to 350 degrees. Spray cookie sheet with nonstick cooking spray.

Blend flour, oats, dry milk and baking powder in food processor, or by hand or with a fork in a large mixing bowl. Mix in milk, peanut butter and molasses. Roll to a ¼-inch thickness and cut or shape as desired using cookie cutter or hands. Place treats on prepared sheet. Bake 20 minutes. Cool in oven and then remove.

Store baked treats in an airtight container or plastic bag and place in refrigerator or freezer. (These freeze well.)

Crunchy, dry cookies are good for a pet's teeth since they remove tartar. After the recommended cooking time, turn off the heat and leave the cookies in the oven 10-15 minutes (up to overnight) or as indicated by the recipe.

Kitty Cuisine

Ham It Up!

Cousin Arthur's quivers of delight are not an act when my people-sister Susan gives him "Ham It Ups." Beef or chicken baby food may be substituted for ham baby food.

Yield: 2½-3 dozen treats

1 jar (2½ ounces) strained ham baby food
¾ cup wheat germ
¾ cup powdered dry milk
1 egg, beaten

Preheat oven to 350 degrees. Spray cookie sheet with nonstick cooking spray.

Mix baby food, wheat germ, dry milk and egg together in a medium mixing bowl. Drop by ½ teaspoonful on prepared sheet. Bake 12-15 minutes. Remove treats from oven and cool on a wire rack. Store baked treats in an airtight container or plastic bag and place in refrigerator or freezer.

The beaten egg used in many recipes may be prepared by breaking an egg into a small bowl and beating it with a fork.

Rice Is Nice

Even Morris would think this was a great treat to munch when watching TV with his people-family.

Yield: 3½-4 cups

2 cups beef broth
1 cup brown rice
1-2 tablespoons cooking oil

Preheat oven to 400 degrees.

Bring broth to a boil in a medium-sized pot. Stir in rice. Return to boiling; simmer 40 minutes or until liquid is absorbed. Spread mixture on ungreased cookie sheet. Bake until rice is brown and crackly (about 15 minutes). Remove from oven.

Heat the oil in a large skillet. Add rice ½ cup at a time and stir until grains puff (3-5 minutes). Drain and then cool on paper towel. Place rice in an airtight container and store in refrigerator.

We used to have a cat, Princess. She sort of liked me, and sometimes we would rub noses. Our new cat, Arthur, isn't fond of me. If we make treats for him, maybe he'll be friendly.

Shrimply Irresistible

There is a rumor that both cats and dogs find this treat irresistible. I can attest to that!

Yield: 2½-3 dozen crescents

1 can (4½ ounces) shrimp, with liquid
1 egg, beaten
2 cups cooked brown rice
½ cup powdered dry milk

Preheat oven to 350 degrees. Spray cookie sheet with nonstick cooking spray.

Chop shrimp in food processor. Add egg; mix well. Blend in rice and dry milk, using on/off pulses. Form into 1½-inch crescent shapes for "shrimp." Place on prepared sheet. Bake 15 minutes. Remove from oven. Let cool completely before removing from sheet. Store baked treats in an airtight container and place in refrigerator or freezer.

On/off pulses of a food processor occur when the mixing action is on for about 5 seconds and then turned off and this is done several times in succession.

Happy as a Clam

The name says it all! Arthur would do a back flip jumping for these yummies.

Yield: 2-2½ dozen treats

1 cup whole wheat bread crumbs	1 can minced clams, drained
¼ cup wheat germ	2 tablespoons clam liquid
½ teaspoon onion powder	1 egg, beaten
2 tablespoons cooking oil	

Preheat oven to 350 degrees. Spray cookie sheet with nonstick cooking spray.

Blend bread crumbs, wheat germ and onion powder in a large mixing bowl. Add oil, clams, clam liquid and egg. Mix well, using hands. Roll into small balls or drop by ½ teaspoonful on prepared sheet. Bake 15 minutes. Cool 20 minutes in oven. Remove treats from oven. Store baked treats in an airtight container or plastic bag in refrigerator or freezer.

Arthur, my people-sister Susan's cat, has been known to actually do a back flip in the air when chasing a snack or toy.

Say Cheese, Please

These delicious morsels will bring a photogenic smile to any cat's face!

Yield: 5-6 dozen treats

6 tablespoons margarine, softened
½ cup grated cheese (room temperature)
1 cup unbleached flour
¼ teaspoon garlic powder
1 tablespoon water

Blend margarine, cheese, flour, garlic powder and water in a medium-sized mixing bowl. Shape into three 6-inch-long logs. Chill 1 hour.

Preheat oven to 375 degrees. Spray cookie sheet with nonstick cooking spray.

Slice into ¼-inch-thick slices. Place slices onto prepared sheet. Bake 10-15 minutes. Remove treats from oven and cool on a wire rack. Store baked treats in an airtight container in freezer.

Unbleached, whole wheat, rye and soy flour, along with cornmeal, rolled oats and wheat germ make pet treats more nutritious.

Pack 'em in: Sardines

Pack 'em in; slam 'em down—that's the way these tidbits will disappear, and that's no fish story!

Yield: 1½-2 dozen treats

1 can (3¾ ounces) sardines, packed in olive oil, drained, reserving 2 tablespoons oil
1 cup whole wheat bread crumbs
1 egg, beaten
½ teaspoon brewer's yeast

Preheat oven to 325 degrees. Spray cookie sheet with nonstick cooking spray.

Mash sardines in a large bowl with reserved oil. Add bread crumbs, egg and brewer's yeast; mix well. Drop by teaspoonful on prepared sheet. Bake 7 minutes. Remove treats from oven and cool on a wire rack. Crumble to serve. Store baked treats in an airtight container and place in refrigerator or freezer.

Preservatives are not used to maintain freshness in pet treats, but treats keep well in the freezer for 6-9 months.

Kitty Had a Little Lamb

The ultimate Pied Piper! Everywhere this lamb goes, the cats are sure to follow.

Yield: 2-2½ dozen treats

½ cup powdered dry milk
⅓ cup wheat germ
⅓ cup soy flour
¼ teaspoon onion or garlic powder

1 egg, beaten
1 tablespoon cooking oil
1 jar (2½ ounces) strained lamb baby food

Preheat oven to 350 degrees. Spray cookie sheet with nonstick cooking spray.

Combine dry milk, wheat germ, flour and onion powder in food processor or with a fork in a large mixing bowl. Add egg, oil and baby food; mix well. Drop by ½ teaspoonful on prepared sheet. Bake 12-15 minutes. Remove treats from oven and cool on a wire rack. Store baked treats in an airtight container in freezer.

Wheat germ contains vitamins and minerals that are beneficial to pets: potassium, iron, folate, zinc, thiamin, phosphorus, and vitamin E.

Eat Your Veggies

Brewer's yeast for your coat and carrots for your eyes...and so good! Two-thirds cup mashed peas may be substituted for the carrots.

Yield: 25 squares

1½ cups whole wheat flour	⅔ cup grated carrots
⅓ cup unbleached flour	1 egg, beaten
⅓ cup cornmeal	⅓ cup water
1 teaspoon brewer's yeast	⅓ cup cooking oil

Preheat oven to 350 degrees. Spray 9x9-inch baking pan with non-stick cooking spray.

Mix flours, cornmeal and yeast together in a large mixing bowl. Add carrots, egg, water and oil; blend well. Spread in prepared pan. Bake for 25 minutes. Remove from oven and cool on a wire rack. Cut in small squares using a cookie cutter or knife. Crumble to serve. Store baked treats in an airtight container and place in refrigerator or freezer.

Brewer's yeast contains several vitamins and minerals which promote pets having healthy skin and coats, and it reduces shedding.

Holy Mackerel

Wow! My cousin Ginger thought she'd died and gone to heaven after tasting these.

Yield: 2½-3 dozen balls

1   can (15 ounces) mackerel, drained and mashed
½   teaspoon onion powder
1   cup whole wheat bread crumbs
2   tablespoons cooking oil
1   egg, beaten

Preheat oven to 350 degrees. Spray cookie sheet with nonstick cooking spray.

In a large bowl, mix mackerel, onion powder, bread crumbs, oil and egg together using hands or on/off pulses of food processor. Drop by teaspoonful or form into 1-inch balls; flatten with fork. Place treats on prepared sheet and bake 20 minutes. Cool in oven and then remove. Crumble to serve. Store baked treats in a plastic bag and place in refrigerator or freezer.

On a hot summer day, I love to "fish" in the shady water under our pier. Once in a while, I catch a minnow.

Here's the Beef!

Smart kitties will have no "beef" with these extra special goodies. Dogs like them too—just ask our friend, Cajun!

Yield: 2-2½ dozen strips

¼ cup powdered dry milk
1½ cups whole wheat flour
¼ teaspoon garlic powder
1 egg, beaten

½ teaspoon powdered beef
   or chicken bouillon
3 tablespoons cooking oil
¼ cup cold water

Preheat oven to 350 degrees. Spray cookie sheet with nonstick cooking spray.

In a large mixing bowl, blend powdered milk, flour and garlic powder with a fork. In a separate bowl, mix egg with bouillon, oil and water. Add to dry ingredients; mix well. Spread on prepared sheet. Cut into ¼-inch strips. Bake 20 minutes. Remove sheet from oven; cool treats on a wire rack. Break into pieces. Store baked treats in an airtight container or plastic bag and place in refrigerator or freezer.

Sometimes we "babysit" our neighbor dog Shadow. She likes to roam, but she comes home lickety-split when my people-mom calls, "Shadow...COOKIES!"

Live It Up Liver

Kitty, my people-grandma's cat, likes these yummy nibbles so much, she jumps down from grandma's lap to get them!

Yield: 2-2½ dozen balls

½ cup pureed, cooked chicken liver with broth
    (see Getting Started)
½ cup powdered dry milk
¾ cup whole grain cereal, crushed
¼ teaspoon onion powder

Preheat oven to 350 degrees. Spray cookie sheet with nonstick cooking spray.

Mix chicken liver mixture, dry milk, cereal and onion powder together in a large mixing bowl. Drop by ½ teaspoonful or shape into ½-inch balls on prepared sheet. Flatten with a fork. Bake 10-12 minutes or until lightly browned. Remove from oven and cool on a wire rack. Crumble to serve. Store baked treats in an airtight container or plastic bag and place in refrigerator or freezer.

Each morning our neighbor dog Shadow waits outside our door so that she can go jogging with me and my people-mom Martha. I wonder if Shadow likes jogging as well as the post-jog treats.

Cat Nippers

A "nip" of this zippy treat isn't enough, according to my cousin Nick.

Yield: 15-18 strips

1 cup whole wheat flour
2 tablespoons wheat germ
1/4 cup soy flour
1/3 cup powdered dry milk

1 teaspoon crushed dry catnip leaves
1 egg, beaten
1 tablespoon molasses
3 tablespoons cooking oil

Preheat oven to 350 degrees. Spray cookie sheet with nonstick cooking spray.

Mix wheat flour, wheat germ, soy flour, dry milk and catnip leaves in a large mixing bowl. Add egg, molasses and oil; mix well. Roll or pat on prepared sheet. Cut into narrow strips. Bake 20 minutes, or until lightly browned. Remove from oven and cool on a wire rack. Break into small pieces to serve. Store baked treats in a plastic bag in freezer.

The herb catnip may be grown in the garden and dried for use, or it may be purchased in pet food supply stores.

That's Corny!

It's not a joke; kitties will do silly tricks if this cornbread treat awaits them!

Yield: 25 squares

1 cup cornmeal
1 cup whole wheat flour
2 tablespoons sugar
1/2 teaspoon baking soda

1 beaten egg
1 cup buttermilk
1/2 cup whole kernel corn, drained

Preheat oven to 400 degrees. Spray 8x8-inch baking pan with non-stick cooking spray.

Blend cornmeal, flour, sugar and soda in a large mixing bowl. Add egg, buttermilk and corn. Mix well with a fork or wooden spoon. Pour into prepared pan. Bake 20-25 minutes. Remove from oven and cool on a wire rack. Cut in small squares. Crumble to serve. Store baked treats in an airtight container and place in refrigerator.

Available in food stores, powdered buttermilk may be stored indefinitely in the refrigerator after opening. The quantity needed is mixed with water at the time of baking.

One Potato, Two Potato

Even pets are into flavored mashed potatoes these days. Mom can use her leftovers for these morsels.

Yield: 2½-3 dozen treats

1 small package (3 ounces) Neufchatel cheese, softened
1 egg, beaten
2 tablespoons flour
½ teaspoon onion powder
⅓ cup shredded carrots (optional)
3 cups cooked, mashed potatoes

Preheat oven to 375 degrees. Spray cookie sheet with nonstick cooking spray.

Mix cheese, egg, flour and onion powder well in a large mixing bowl using a wooden spoon. Add carrots and potatoes; mix well. Drop by rounded teaspoonful on prepared sheet. Bake 15 minutes or until lightly browned. Remove from oven. Cool completely before removing from cookie sheet. Store baked treats in an airtight container and place in refrigerator.

Some cats prefer food in small pieces. This and most cat treats may be crumbled for serving.

Puddy-Cat Casserole

This will need a "No People Allowed" sign on it when it is in the refrigerator.

Yield: one 8x8-inch casserole

1½ cups cooked noodles or spaghetti
1 can (15 ounces) salmon, drained
¼ teaspoon onion powder
2 tablespoons cooking oil
½ cup plain yogurt

Preheat oven to 350 degrees. Spray 8x8-inch baking pan with non-stick cooking spray.

Chop noodles in food processor. In a separate small bowl, mash salmon with a fork. Add salmon, onion powder, oil and yogurt to the noodles; mix well. Spread in prepared pan. Bake 30 minutes. Remove from oven and cool on a wire rack. Cut into small squares. Crumble to serve. Store baked treats in an airtight container and place in refrigerator or freezer.

I have perfected "the look" in my quest for snacks. A cocked head, furrowed brow, and forlorn eyes will win over the most skeptical human.

Index of Recipes

K

L

M

O

P

R

S

T

Y